To my niblings who love spiders and wanted to tell me about their favorite spider—the Goliath birdeater.

Published by Larch Books, Portland, Oregon
Library of Congress Control Number: 2020909383
ISBN 978-1-946748-11-9 (hc), 978-1-946748-12-6 (pbk)

For more information, visit www.aesauble.com.

Can a Spider Be Fluffy?

Written and illustrated by
Audrey Sauble

Have you ever stopped to watch
a spider? Was it fluffy or smooth?
Spotted or plain?

What did it look like?

Well . . .

What do yellow garden spiders look like? Are they fluffy?

No, yellow garden spiders look smooth and elegant.

These spiders often add a zigzag pattern to their webs. ➜

What about nursery web spiders?
Do they look fluffy?

Nursery web spiders look thin
and pointy.

Nursery web spiders build special nests for their spiderlings. ➔

Giant house spiders don't look fluffy either. They look long and skinny, just like . . .

. . . a daddy longlegs.

Wait! This is the wrong one!
This daddy longlegs can't spin
silk. This is a harvestman,
not a spider.

Harvestmen only have two eyes.
Spiders have four to eight eyes.

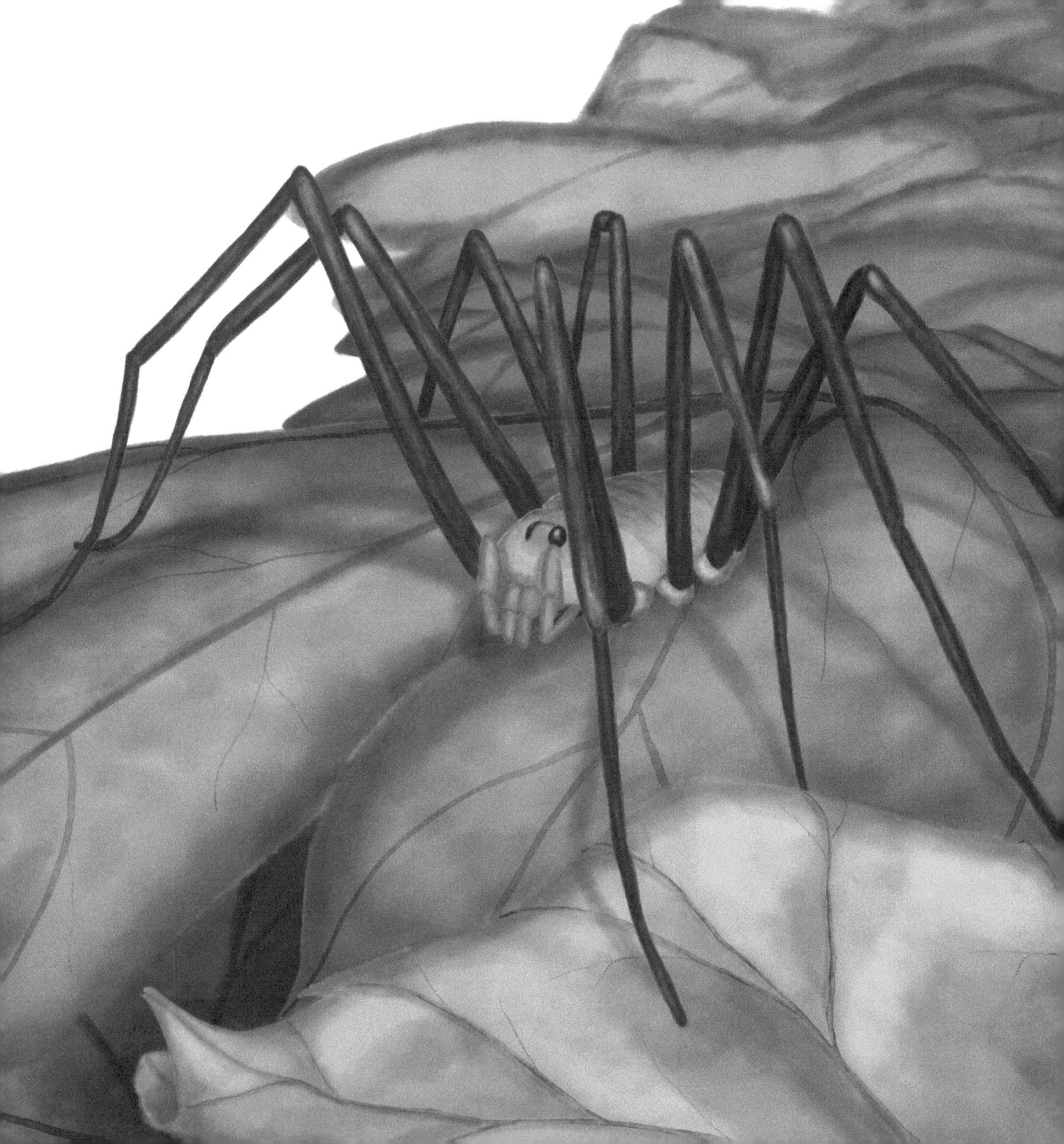

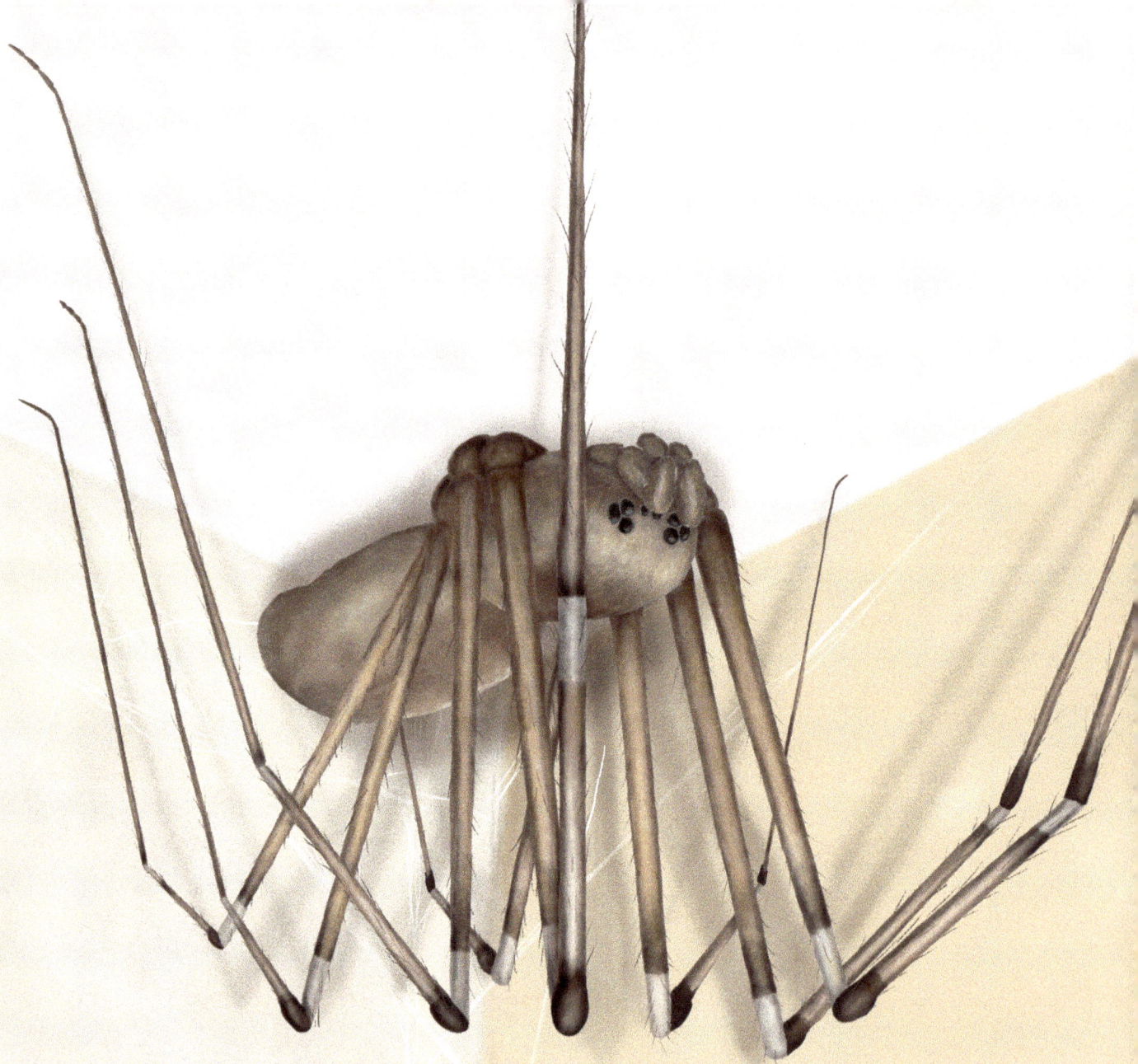

This daddy longlegs is a spider, though. Does it look fluffy?

No, it looks thin and scraggly.

← These spiders are also called cellar spiders.

Are any spiders fluffy?

Cross spiders have bristles
all over their legs, but they
aren't fluffy.

Cross spiders build a frame for their web with
nonsticky silk, then add sticky silk to trap insects.

Barn spiders are a bit shaggy, but they look more prickly than fluffy.

← **Many spiders like to hide their egg sacs in dark corners.**

And bolas spiders don't look fluffy at all. They look swollen and lumpy.

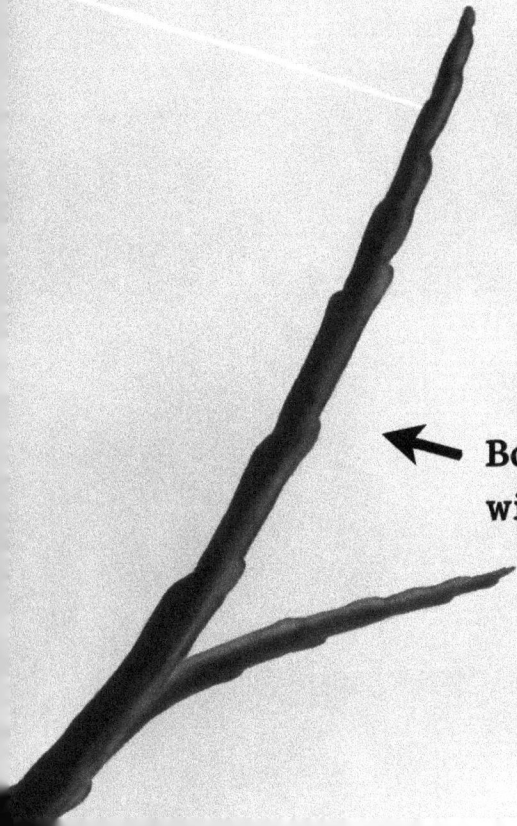

← Bolas spiders catch moths with a sticky spitball.

What about spiny orb-weavers?
Do they look fluffy?

Spiny orb-weavers look spiky.

← These spiders come in several different bright colors.

Crab spiders look soft and plump, but they don't look fluffy.

Crab spiders hide in flowers instead of building a web. →

And ant mimics don't even look like spiders. Can you guess what they do look like?

These spiders sometimes wave their front legs in the air to make their legs look like antennae.

Are cobweb spiders fluffy?

No, cobweb spiders are round and shiny.

← Cobweb spiders are related to black widow spiders, but they aren't dangerous to humans.

Wolf spiders aren't fluffy either. They are hairy, but their hair looks sleek and flat, not fuzzy.

← These spiders look after their spiderlings for a couple of weeks after they hatch.

Still, some spiders can look a bit fluffy. Jumping spiders look almost cuddly.

Jumping spiders are about the size of an ant in real life. ➤

And Goliath birdeater tarantulas look fluffy as well, especially their thick, furry legs.

But . . .

Actual size—Goliath birdeaters are one of the largest spiders in the world.

... Even jumping spiders and Goliath birdeaters aren't as fluffy as a pink-toed tarantula.

Pink-toed tarantulas might be the fluffiest spider in the world. What do you think? →

Did you know? This book uses the spiders' common names because those are the ones most people would usually recognize.

However, different species of spiders sometimes share common names. For example, tarantulas got their name from a species of European spider—but that spider is a type of wolf spider. This can make it confusing to discuss spiders using their common names.

That's why scientists use scientific names for spiders—and other animals! Can you match these spiders' scientific names with their common names?

Steatoda triangulosa

Eris militaris

Argiope aurantia

Araneus cavaticus

Eratigena duellica

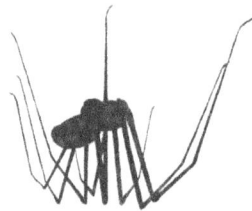

Pholcus phalangioides

Pisaurina mira

Araneus diadematus

Synemosyna formica

Misumena vatia

Mastaphora hutchinsoni

Gasteracantha cancriformis

Are spiders dangerous? Yes—if you are a bug!

Spiders just want to find food and stay safe. Most spiders probably think you are scary! Some spiders may bite humans, though, if they feel threatened.

Have an adult help you research which spiders in your area may be dangerous. Then draw a picture of those spiders so you know which ones to avoid.

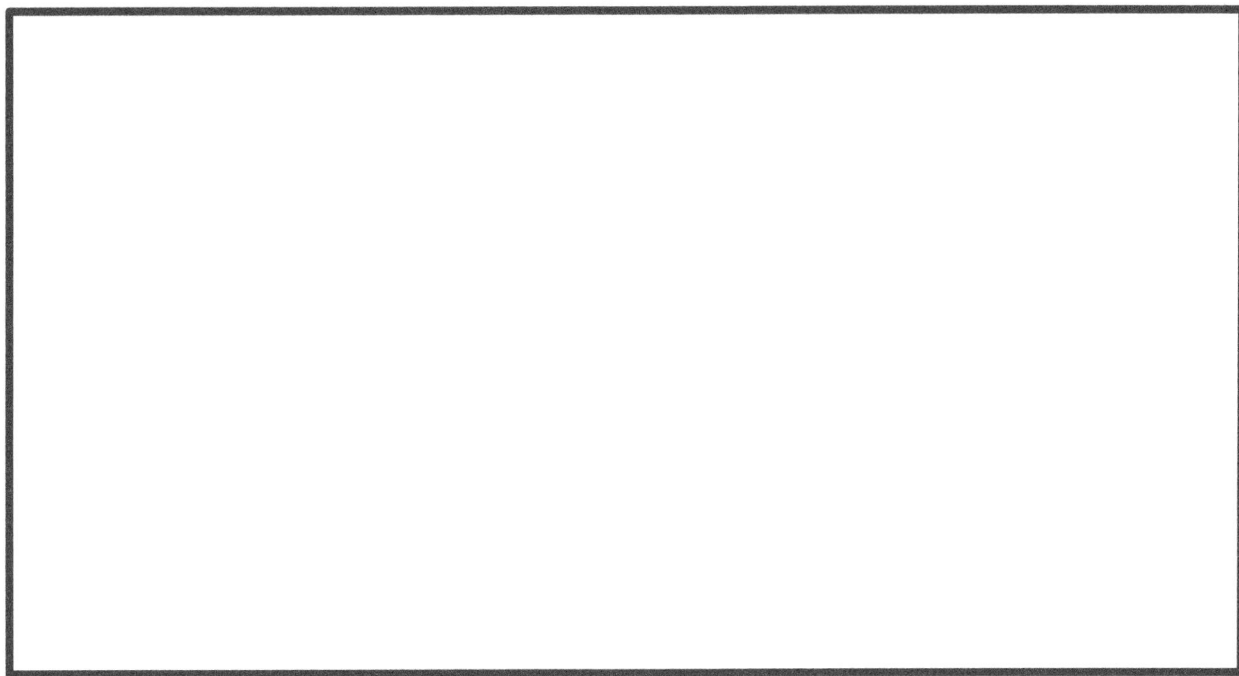

Hunt and find: Orb weavers are a family of spiders who usually build round webs. Five of the spiders in this book are orb weavers. Can you figure out which ones those are? (*Hint: one is the same species as a spider in a famous children's book. Another one uses a tiny, sticky ball to catch moths.*)

www.ingramcontent.com/pod-product-compliance
Lightning Source LLC
Chambersburg PA
CBHW051322020426
42333CB00031B/3442